# DISCOVERING ENDANGERED SPECIES

W9-BZX-614

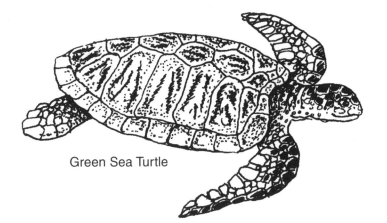

Green Sea Turtle

## By
## Nancy Field
## Sally Machlis

Illustrated by Sally Machlis

Cover art by Michael Maydak

Copyright © 1990 Dog-Eared Publications

Cover art copyright © 1999 Michael Maydak

Fifth Printing 1999

P.O. Box 620863, Middleton, WI 53562-0863; Web Site: http://www.dog-eared.com

ISBN 0-941042-09-X

 *Printed in the USA on Recycled Paper with Soy Ink*

# Have You Ever Wondered?

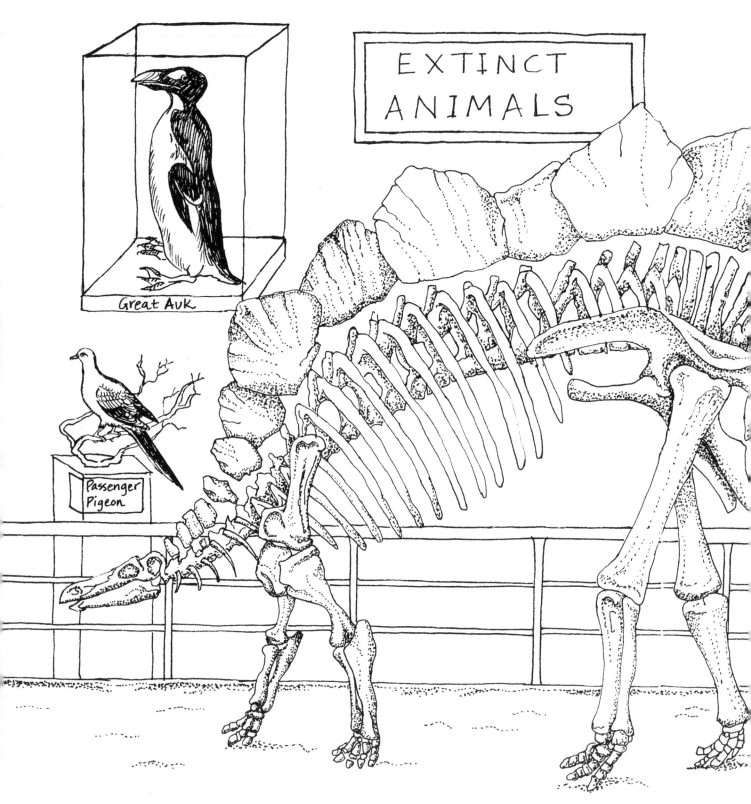

- Why did dinosaurs become extinct?

- What is the difference between extinct, endangered, and threatened?

- Does it matter if an animal or plant becomes extinct?

- Why are animals and plants in danger?

- What do animals and plants need in order to stay alive?

- Is an ant as important as an elephant?

- Is a small flower as important as a big tree?

- How many kinds of living things live in our world?

- What makes some plants and animals more at risk than others?

- What is being done to help save endangered species?
- How can I help?

As you read this book, you will find the answers to these questions and many others. You will learn what you, your family, friends, and class can do to help save endangered species.

STEGOSAURUS

DoDo

# Disappearing Act

Up to thirty-three million **species** or kinds of animals, plants, and other life share this earth. No one knows the exact number for sure. All over the world, many are becoming extinct.

**Extinct** animals and plants are species that are gone forever. They once lived on earth but have died out.

Tyrannosaurus

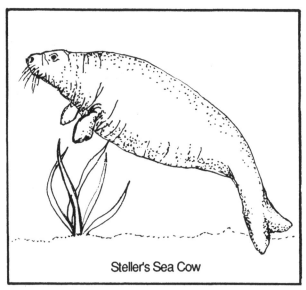

Steller's Sea Cow

### Caused by Nature

Since life on Earth began, plants and animals have come and gone. Changes in nature caused their extinction. Why did dinosaurs become extinct? There are several ideas. Comets, asteroids, or volcanoes might have caused a rapid change in climate. Or perhaps dinosaurs disappeared slowly. Over millions of years, their surroundings might have changed. Have you heard of other reasons?

### Caused by Humans

The growing numbers of people cause problems for other life on earth. As the human population grows, more and more species become extinct. Steller's sea cows were hunted to extinction by people. There is a difference between nature-caused and human-caused extinctions. We can do something about our actions.

## Journey to Extinction

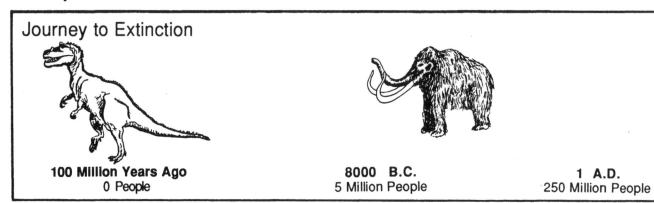

**100 Million Years Ago**
0 People

8000  B.C.
5 Million People

1  A.D.
250 Million People

**Endangered** plants and animals are still living today but are in immediate danger of extinction. Thousands of species are now endangered.

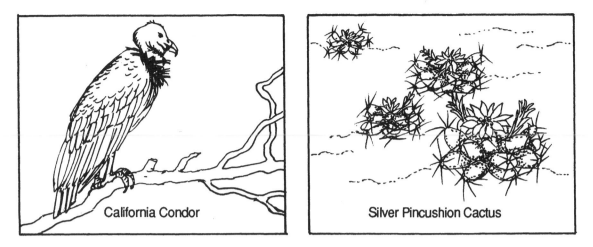

California Condor

Silver Pincushion Cactus

**Threatened** species have low or declining population numbers. There are very few of them left. They are not endangered now, but are likely to become so in the future if not protected.

Snail Darter

Northern Monkshood

More species become extinct each year. Scientists think that now we lose species every single day! This is all the more reason to think of ways to help.

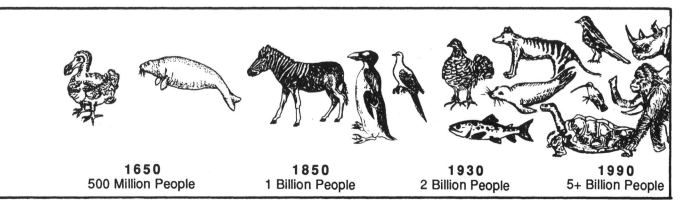

**1650**
500 Million People

**1850**
1 Billion People

**1930**
2 Billion People

**1990**
5+ Billion People

# The Earth's Gifts

Plants and animals are valuable to people. Thousands are useful to us in our everyday lives because they provide food or other products. Others are important just because they exist and give us pleasure. **Use the secret code to fill in the boxes below with the correct letter. The first one is done for you. You will find reasons plants and animals are valuable to us.**

Secret Code:

| 1 | 2 | 3 | 4 | 5 | 6 | 7 | 8 | 9 | 10 | 11 | 12 | 13 | 14 | 15 | 16 | 17 | 18 | 19 | 20 | 21 | 22 | 23 | 24 | 25 | 26 |
|---|---|---|---|---|---|---|---|---|----|----|----|----|----|----|----|----|----|----|----|----|----|----|----|----|----|
| A | B | C | D | E | F | G | H | I | J | K | L | M | N | O | P | Q | R | S | T | U | V | W | X | Y | Z |

A.

| 6 F | 15 O | 15 O | 4 D |
|---|---|---|---|

B.

| 16 | 18 | 15 | 4 | 21 | 3 | 20 | 19 |
|---|---|---|---|---|---|---|---|

C.

| 18 | 5 | 3 | 18 | 5 | 1 | 20 | 9 | 15 | 14 |
|---|---|---|---|---|---|---|---|---|---|

D.

| 13 | 5 | 4 | 9 | 3 | 9 | 14 | 5 |
|---|---|---|---|---|---|---|---|

E.

| 6 | 21 | 5 | 12 |
|---|---|---|---|

F.

| 3 | 12 | 15 | 20 | 8 | 5 | 19 |
|---|---|---|---|---|---|---|

G.

| 6 | 5 | 18 | 20 | 9 | 12 | 9 | 26 | 5 |
|---|---|---|---|---|---|---|---|---|

| 6 | 12 | 15 | 23 · | 5 | 18 | 19 |
|---|---|---|---|---|---|---|

H.

| 2 | 5 | 1 | 21 | 20 | 25 |
|---|---|---|---|---|---|

I.

| 13 | 1 | 11 | 5 |
|---|---|---|---|

| 15 | 24 | 25 | 7 | 5 | 14 |
|---|---|---|---|---|---|

Can you think of any other ways plants and animals are of value to people? Some species may become extinct before we can identify them and learn of their value. We won't even know what we are losing.

Answers on last page

# Bricks of the Earth

Living things come in millions of shapes, sizes, and colors. They live in many different kinds of places. Scientists call all this variety **biological diversity.** Each animal or plant, large or small, has its own special role to play in the way the world works. These plants and animals are all connected, and they depend on each other. Sometimes the connections can't be seen and are difficult to understand.

All this variety matters. Losing a species from the world is like taking a brick out of a house. If you take one away, it can weaken the whole. **Color the bricks in the house below. Start with number one and color the bricks in order.** Think of each colored brick as a species becoming extinct. How many species can disappear before the house will fall down?

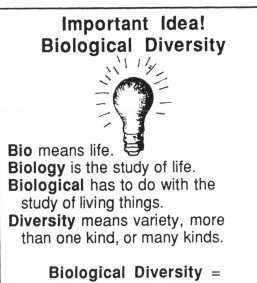

**Important Idea!
Biological Diversity**

**Bio** means life.
**Biology** is the study of life.
**Biological** has to do with the study of living things.
**Diversity** means variety, more than one kind, or many kinds.

**Biological Diversity** =
Variety of living things

# What Do Living Things Need?

How are animals like people? Like you, they also need **food** and **water**. They need **shelter** just as you need a home. They must have space around their shelter just as you need a neighborhood. The place where an animal lives and finds its needs is called a **habitat**. Here everything is arranged in a way that makes it possible for the animal to live.

Plants have needs also. They must have the proper amount of **sunlight**, clean **air** and **water**, along with the right kind of **soil**. They make their own food using these materials. Plants also need space to grow.

One reason our planet has so many kinds of animals and plants is its great variety of habitats - - forests, grasslands, wetlands and deserts are a few. Habitats can also become endangered. **Can you help these animals and plants find their needs in this endangered old growth forest? Place the numbers in the correct spaces.** Some spaces could have more than one number. You might find some surprises.

Spotted Owl
_____ Food
_____ Water
_____ Nest Site

Hemlock Seedling
_____ Place to Grow
_____ Place to get Nutrients
_____ Water

Salamander
_____ Food
_____ Water
_____ Shelter

False Lady's Slipper
_____ Place to Grow
_____ Place to get Nutrients
_____ Water

Flying Squirrel
_____ Food
_____ Water
_____ Nest Site

Answers on last page

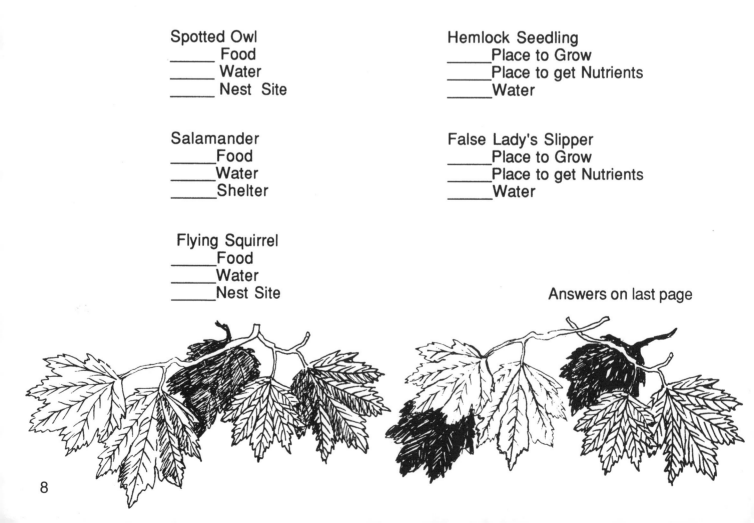

6 Red Tree Vole

1 Cavity in Top of Snag

2

Spotted Owl

5 Northern Flying Squirrel

15 Douglas-fir Tree

2 Cavities in Living Tree or Snag

14 Hemlock Seedling

9 Stream

8 Mite

Snag (A Dead Tree)

3 Rotting Fallen Log Full of Moisture

4 Pool of Water

11 Slender Salamander

12 Truffle (Underground Mushroom)

13 False Lady's Slipper

7 Collembolan (An Insect)

10 soil

9

# What Goes Wrong?
## Habitat Loss

There are many reasons that a plant or animal might become threatened, endangered, or extinct. Habitat loss is the main reason. Habitat is lost when it is changed or destroyed. The new habitat often isn't suitable for animals and plants that lived there before.

**What has happened in each of the pictures below that caused the loss of the original habitat? Write your answer on the lines below the picture.**

A. _____ Original _____

_____ Habitat _____

B. _____

_____

C. _____

_____

D. _____

_____

E. _____

_____

F. _____

_____

Answers on last page

Many habitats, like old growth forests, are disappearing. Let's look at some others. The following pages about habitat loss have this special symbol:

10

# Habitat Loss in Bamboo Forests of China

The bamboo forest of China is the habitat of the giant panda. The forests were cut to make room for houses, villages, and crops. As bamboo disappears, there is not enough food and shelter for pandas. Only a few isolated places are left for them in western China.

**Giant Panda**

Length: close to 5 feet (1.5 meters)

Weight: up to 260 pounds (117 kg)

Color: black and white

Food: mainly bamboo, 22 to 44 pounds a day (10 to 20 kg), occasionally other plants and mammals

Habitat: bamboo and evergreen forests of China

Reasons Endangered: habitat loss, poaching, needs special diet of bamboo

# Habitat Loss in Grasslands

Once fields of grasses and flowers, called **prairies**, stretched across a large part of North America. When pioneers came, these grasslands were plowed under for crops like corn and wheat. Fires, which prairie plants needed for survival, were stopped. Native animals, like bison, pronghorn antelope, and prairie-dogs, were replaced by cattle, sheep, and horses. Today there are few real prairies left.

Grasslands are found all over the world. They have wonderful names like savannas, pampas, and steppes. Problems similar to those in North America have caused habitat loss in these places. Today, fewer than half the earth's grasslands remain.

### Black Footed Ferret

Length: up to 2 feet (61 cm)
including tail, males larger

Weight: up to 2 1/2 pounds
(about 1 kg)

Color: black face mask, feet and tail tip;
yellow-buff body with white on
forehead, muzzle and throat

Food: mainly prairie dogs

Habitat: prairies of North America

Reasons Endangered: loss of food, habitat loss

### Wild Petunia

Height: 2 to 3 feet (almost 1 meter)

Color: blue, magenta, gray or white

Habitat: prairies from eastern U.S. to Nebraska,
south to Texas

Reason Endangered: habitat loss

# Habitat Loss in Deserts

Deserts are not just barren, sandy areas. Some natural deserts are full of life. These plants and animals are adapted to desert habitats. They have special ways of dealing with the dry and often hot conditions.

There are many reasons living deserts change into lifeless wastelands. Overgrazing by cattle and sheep destroys plants. The desert habitat is lost as cities and roads are built. Dune buggies and other off-road vehicles kill plants and animals. Mining operations remove soil and destroy plants. With fewer plants, the desert soil erodes away. Native plants usually can't grow back once the desert soil is gone. Like other habitats, deserts also need protection.

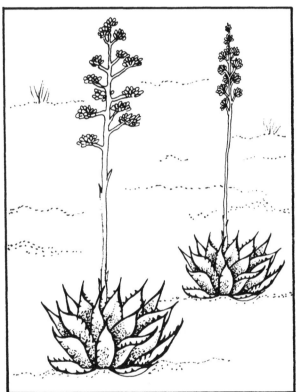

**Lesser Long-nosed Bat**
(Formerly Sanborn's Long-nosed Bat)

Length:  up to 3 1/2 inches (90 mm)
wingspan 10 inches (254 mm)

Weight: 18 to 30 grams

Color:  brownish

Food:  with 3 inch-long tongues they eat nectar and pollen from flowers of desert plants like the agave and the saguaro cactus; fruit and insects

Habitat:  summer in deserts and desert grasslands of Arizona and New Mexico; winter in various habitats of Central America

Reasons Endangered:  habitat loss, disturbance of roost sights, killed as pest, loss of food plants

**Arizona Agave or Century Plant**

Height:  up to 11 inches (30 cm) flower stalk up to 13 feet (3 to 4 meters)

Width:  up to 15 inches (40 cm)

Flowers: bloom only once in plant's lifetime

Color:  dark green leaves, pale yellow flowers

Habitat:  found from 3000 to 4000 feet high in Arizona chaparral (an area with low, shrubby plants) and juniper grassland

Reasons Endangered:  collecting, habitat damage - especially cattle grazing

# Habitat Loss in Rain Forests South and Central America

Half of all plant and animal species on earth live in tropical rain forests. Nowhere is there more variety of life, or biological diversity. These rain forests are quickly disappearing. One reason is the demand for products. Trees, such as mahogany and rosewood, are cut to make items like furniture, boats and toys. Forests have been cleared for farmland and cattle ranches. Trees are often cut at the rate of 50 acres a minute. (That's about 45 football fields every single minute!) Forest loss causes the extinction of other life. Scientists will not have enough time to learn about or even name all the species before they are extinct.

**Find the following endangered species in this picture.**

| | | | |
|---|---|---|---|
| Three-toed sloth | Wooly spider monkey | Jaguar | Golden lion tamarin |
| Giant otter | Buff-headed marmoset | Ocelot | Scarlet macaw |
| Giant anteater | Thin-spined porcupine | Caiman | |

Answers on last page

# Habitat Loss in Rain Forests of Africa

African rain forests are vanishing also. Many people are building roads and moving into the forests. They are cutting and burning trees for farms and firewood. Often they are poor. Feeding themselves and making a living is difficult.

Africa is home for many of the great apes like gorillas and chimpanzees. Habitat destruction is a serious problem for these animals. As the African rain forest disappears, these creatures have less and less habitat.

**Mountain Gorilla**

Length: male up to 5 feet 7 inches
(1.7 meters)
female up to 4 feet 7 inches
(1.4 meters)

Weight: males up to 343 pounds (156 kg)
females up to 175 pounds (79 kg)

Color: jet black, adult males have silvery white on back between shoulders

Food: leaves, shoots, stems of plants; some wood, roots, flowers, fruit and grubs

Habitat: forests of Central Africa

Reasons Endangered: habitat loss, poaching

**Chimpanzee**

Length: 3.5 to 5.5 feet   (1.6 meters)

Weight: males up to 110 pounds (49.9 kg)
females up to 55 pounds (24.9 kg)

Color: usually black with a white patch near rump; nose, ears, hands and feet flesh colored

Food: fruit, leaves, blossoms, seeds, stems, bark, resin, honey, insects, eggs and meat

Habitat: forests and denser woodlands of Africa

Reasons Endangered: habitat loss, overhunting locally, poaching, collected for animal trade

# Coral Reef Habitat Loss

Coral reefs are found in shallow, tropical water. Corals are living animals. They build outside skeletons to shelter and protect themselves. Each skeleton is cemented to its neighbors. Even after the animal inside dies, its skeleton remains. Over time, these animals construct a large reef which looks like a colorful maze of castles, caves, and canyons. Many kinds of animals and plants find food and shelter here.

Reefs are destroyed when they are dredged to make way for harbors and buildings. Coral is smothered by runoff of soil from construction. Coral, shells, and fish disappear as they are carried off for collectors. Illegal fishermen try to scare fish from their homes. Some use dynamite or poison, destroying the coral. When the coral is destroyed, there is no habitat for other forms of life.

**Unscramble the names of the animals living in this reef.**

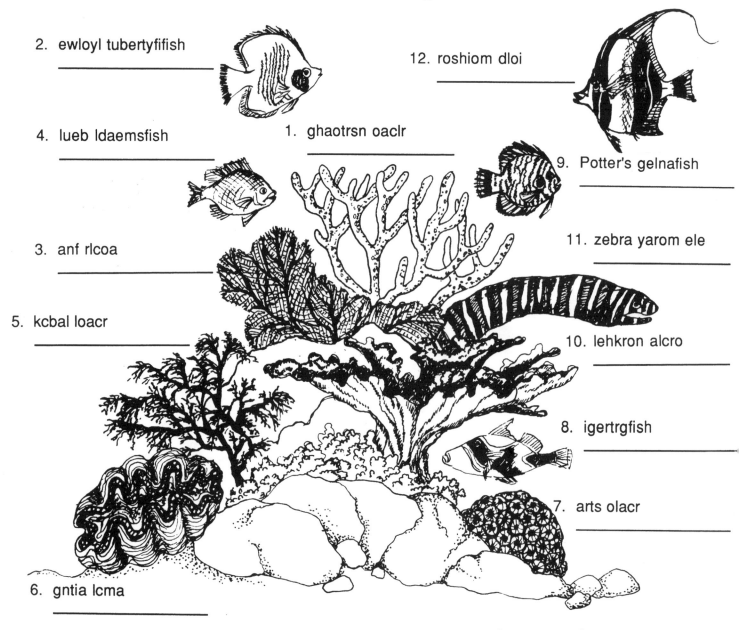

2. ewloyl tubertyfifish

_____

4. lueb ldaemsfish

_____

3. anf rlcoa

_____

5. kcbal loacr

_____

6. gntia lcma

_____

1. ghaotrsn oaclr

_____

12. roshiom dloi

_____

9. Potter's gelnafish

_____

11. zebra yarom ele

_____

10. lehkron alcro

_____

8. igertrgfish

_____

7. arts olacr

_____

Answers on last page

# Wandering Through Wetlands

## A Game About Wetlands and Habitat Loss

Many animals and plants live in wetland habitats. Wetlands are soggy places. At least part of the year, they are covered by shallow water or have waterlogged soil. Some are inland and have fresh water. Others are on ocean coasts and have salt water. Marshes, swamps, prairie potholes, bogs, and mudflats are examples of wetlands.

For a long time people thought wetlands were useless. In the past fifty or more years, people have found ways to change wetlands for their own use. This has caused TROUBLE for wetland creatures. Today, fewer than half of North America's original wetlands remain.

In this game you will learn why wetlands are important. You will also find out ways these habitats are being changed.

### Rules

1.  The object of the game is to be the first player to reach FINISH.

2.  Each player needs to make his or her own playing piece. One way is to find a small pebble that looks different from the other players' markers. Another way would be to trace one of the wetland animals pictured on this page. Color, cut it out, and tape a penny to the back.

3.  Find four objects, such as paper pieces or pebbles. Number them 1,2,3, and 4 using a pencil, crayon, or whatever you can find to make a mark. Place them in a container, like a paper bag or hat. When it is your turn, draw a number and move the correct number of squares. You might also use dice.

4.  Each time you land on a dark space, follow the special instructions on the board.

Turn the page to play the game.

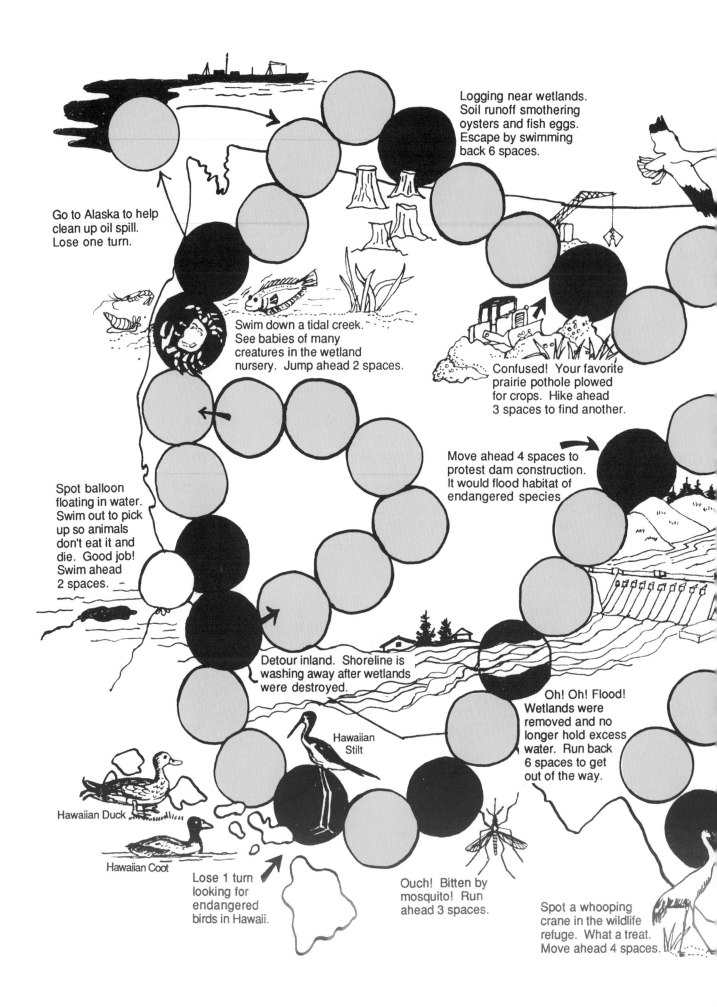

Logging near wetlands. Soil runoff smothering oysters and fish eggs. Escape by swimming back 6 spaces.

Go to Alaska to help clean up oil spill. Lose one turn.

Swim down a tidal creek. See babies of many creatures in the wetland nursery. Jump ahead 2 spaces.

Confused! Your favorite prairie pothole plowed for crops. Hike ahead 3 spaces to find another.

Move ahead 4 spaces to protest dam construction. It would flood habitat of endangered species

Spot balloon floating in water. Swim out to pick up so animals don't eat it and die. Good job! Swim ahead 2 spaces.

Detour inland. Shoreline is washing away after wetlands were destroyed.

Hawaiian Stilt

Oh! Oh! Flood! Wetlands were removed and no longer hold excess water. Run back 6 spaces to get out of the way.

Hawaiian Duck

Hawaiian Coot

Lose 1 turn looking for endangered birds in Hawaii.

Ouch! Bitten by mosquito! Run ahead 3 spaces.

Spot a whooping crane in the wildlife refuge. What a treat. Move ahead 4 spaces.

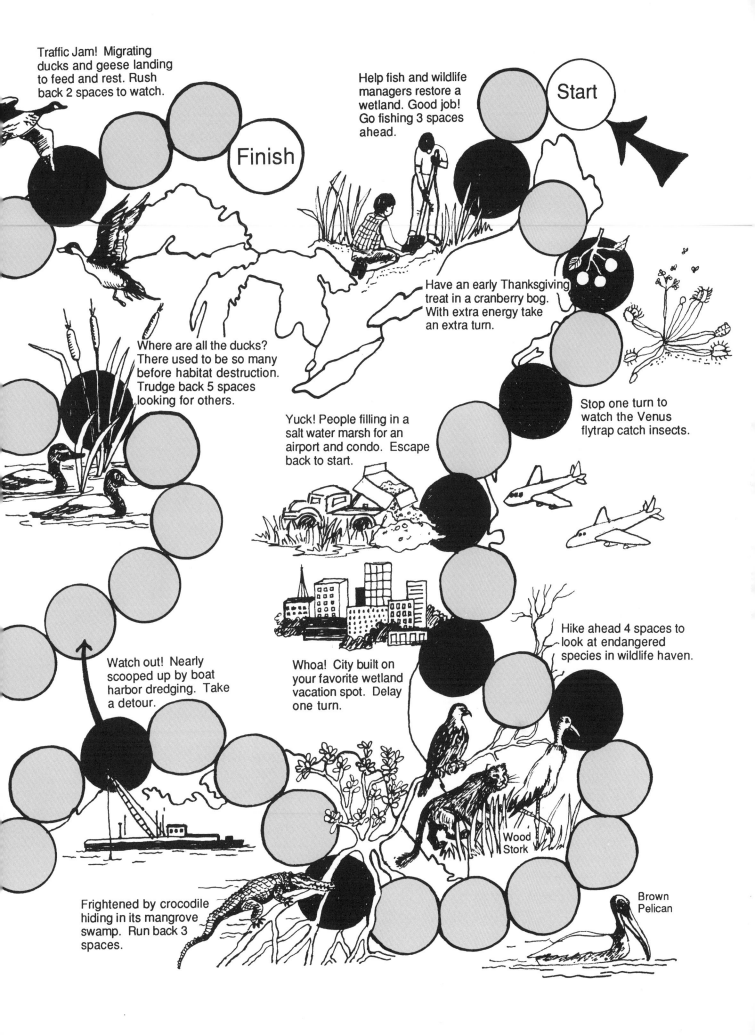

Traffic Jam! Migrating ducks and geese landing to feed and rest. Rush back 2 spaces to watch.

Finish

Help fish and wildlife managers restore a wetland. Good job! Go fishing 3 spaces ahead.

Start

Have an early Thanksgiving treat in a cranberry bog. With extra energy take an extra turn.

Where are all the ducks? There used to be so many before habitat destruction. Trudge back 5 spaces looking for others.

Stop one turn to watch the Venus flytrap catch insects.

Yuck! People filling in a salt water marsh for an airport and condo. Escape back to start.

Hike ahead 4 spaces to look at endangered species in wildlife haven.

Watch out! Nearly scooped up by boat harbor dredging. Take a detour.

Whoa! City built on your favorite wetland vacation spot. Delay one turn.

Wood Stork

Brown Pelican

Frightened by crocodile hiding in its mangrove swamp. Run back 3 spaces.

# Exotic Strangers

Sometimes new animals or plants are brought into an area where they never lived before. They are called **exotic** species. They compete with native species for food, water, shelter and space. Some kill the local animals for food. Exotic species can also bring diseases. With no natural enemies, they grow in numbers at a very fast rate. Rats, goats, pigs, cattle, and rabbits are examples of exotics that have destroyed the original animals and plants.

In Hawaii, rats were accidentally brought to the islands on ships. They ate the eggs of birds. The mongoose was introduced to get rid of the rats. This turned out to be a mistake. The mongoose ate the rats and the bird's eggs too!

### Nene or Hawaiian Goose

Length:  up to 2 ft 4 in (71 cm)

Weight:  to 5 pounds (2.25 kg)
males a little larger

Color:  heavily barred, gray-brown body, buff-colored cheek and neck, black face, head , nape of neck, bill and feet

Food:  berries, grass, leaves, stems and seeds

Habitat:  Islands of Hawaii and Maui, Hawaii

Reasons Endangered:  eaten by exotic species, overhunting

### Little Agate Snails

(A Group of Related Snails)

Length:  up to 1 inch (2.7 cm)

Color:  variously patterned, shades of red, orange, yellow, brown, green, grey, blue, black, and white; each shell is unique

Food:  algae, fungi, liverworts from leaves, and bark

Habitat:  lives in trees and shrubs on Oahu Island, Hawaii

Reasons Endangered:  eaten by exotic species, overcollecting, habitat destruction

# Overhunting

Once, animals such as whales and fur-bearing mammals were plentiful. The numbers of humans were small, so the animals were not overhunted. Most parts of the animals were used for food, clothing , bedding, shelter, and tools.

Later, modern methods allowed people to kill as many animals as they wanted. Sometimes too many animals were killed. This is called overhunting. When there are too few animals, they have trouble finding mates. When there are no offspring, the species faces danger of extinction.

Today, some species like white-tailed deer are abundant and can be hunted. Laws protect these animals from being overhunted. Good hunters obey the laws and act responsibly.

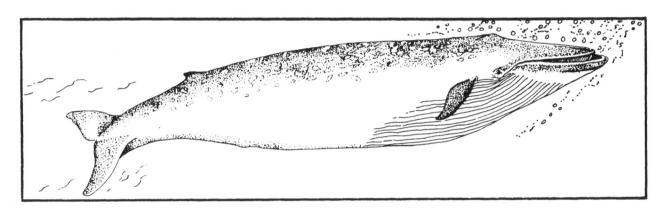

### Blue Whale

Length: up to 100 feet (30 meters)

Weight: up to 360,000 pounds (180 tons)

Color: light bluish gray mottled with grayish white; undersides of flippers lighter color; belly can look yellow

Food: shrimp-like animals

Habitat: Atlantic and Pacific Oceans

Reasons Endangered: overhunting

### Snow Leopard

Length: head and body up to 4.3 feet (1.4 meters)

Weight: up to 165 pounds (75 kg)

Color: pale gray with white underparts; solid spots on head and lower limbs; rings enclose some small spots on body

Food: Sheep, deer, mountain goats, boar, marmots, and domestic livestock

Habitat: high mountains of Central Asia

Reasons Endangered: overhunting, loss of food, killed as pest

# Friend or Foe?

Some animals have been considered dangerous to humans and their property. Tigers, grizzly bears, wolves, rhinoceroses, cougars, bobcats, crocodiles, alligators, and bald eagles are some of the animals that have killed livestock. Occasionally, people have been killed. Elephants and bison are among the animals that have destroyed crops. To protect themselves and their crops, people have shot, poisoned, and trapped these animals. Some governments paid money, called a **bounty**, to people who killed these animals. Now, many of these species have become very rare. They may become extinct unless we make special efforts to save them.

**Gray Wolf**

Length: up to 4 feet (1.2 meters)
tail up to 1.5 feet (48 cm)

Height: 24 to 28 inches (.7 meter)

Weight: males 70 to 120 pounds (54 kg)
females 55 to 90 pounds (40.8 kg)

Color: white to black and every color in between, often light gray or brown sprinkled with black, yellow and white on legs and underparts

Food: often young, old and unhealthy large mammals like deer, elk, moose, mountain goats; beaver, mice, rabbits and ground squirrels

Habitat: all habitats of Northern Hemisphere except tropical forests and dry deserts

Reasons Endangered: killed as pest, overhunting, habitat loss

**Grizzly Bear**

Length: 4 to 6 feet or larger (1.8 meters), females smaller

Height: up to 3.5 feet (1.1 meters)

Weight: from 325 to 850 pounds (385 kg)

Color: ranges from yellowish to dark brown or black, hair frequently tipped with white, giving a frosted grizzled appearance

Food: plants like grasses, roots, bulbs and berries; also salmon, insects, mice, squirrels, marmots; some places moose, elk, mountain goat and even black bears

Habitat: Variety of habitats, often prefers open areas like tundra, alpine meadows and coastlines

Reasons Endangered: killed as pest, overhunting, habitat loss

# Poaching

Some endangered plants and animals are protected by laws. Yet they are still hunted and collected illegally. This is called **poaching**. Ivory or coral jewelry, fur, feathers, teeth, reptile skins, and exotic pets and plants are sold illegally. Sometimes people don't even realize that a product comes from an endangered species.

When people learn that buying ivory and other products bring animals and plants closer to extinction, they may stop buying the products. When no one buys the products, then poaching might stop.

## Black Rhinoceros

Length: body and head up to 12 feet (375 cm)

Height: up to 5 feet (150 cm)

Weight: up to 3960 pounds or 1.9 tons (1800 kg)

Color: dark yellow brown to dark brown or dark gray

Food: bushes and shrubs

Habitat: once found throughout eastern and southern Africa living in areas between grasslands and forests near permanent water holes

Reasons Endangered: poached illegally for horns, habitat loss

## African Elephant

Length: body, head and trunk up to 24 feet (750 cm)

Height: up to 11 1/4 feet (342 cm)

Weight: up to 16500 pounds or 8 tons (7500 kg)

Color: dull brownish gray with sparsely scattered black bristly hairs

Food: grasses, trees, bark and shrubs

Habitat: once found throughout Africa in all habitats

Reasons Endangered: poached illegally for ivory, habitat loss

# Collecting

Collections are fun and educational. Perhaps you know someone who collects stamps, or coins, or books.

Sometimes collectors can cause the extinction of species. Home gardeners may buy rare orchids, cacti, or flower bulbs for their plant collections. They may not even know the plants are endangered. Others may steal rare plants. Butterflies, sea shells, snakes, fish, and coral are also among endangered species often collected. For many, like the butterflies, the problem begins with habitat loss. Once much of the habitat is gone, collecting becomes a threat. Collecting needs to be controlled with good laws.

**Homerus Swallowtail Butterfly**

Length: up to 6 1/2 inches (16.5 cm)

Weight: 1 or 2 grams

Color: upper wing black with yellow, black and red markings; underside chocolate brown

Food: a few species of plants

Habitat: mountain slopes and gullies on the island of Jamaica

Reasons Threatened: mainly habitat loss, collecting

**Nichol's Turk's Head Cactus**
(Devil's Head Cactus)

Height: up to 12 inches (30.5 cm) nearly spherical

Color: blue green pink flowers

Habitat: two desert locations in southern Arizona

Reasons Endangered: overcollecting, habitat loss, mining operations

# Smuggler Story Problem

Using the math you've learned in school, fill in the correct numbers in the missing spaces.

The smugglers are in the jungle. They find a flock of 1000 parrots. They know it is against the law to trap these parrots. Yet, they are willing to risk large fines and jail to make money. Using nets, they capture 1/2 of the birds. They have caught _____ birds. Of these, 200 birds are injured and die, leaving _____ birds. Shock kills 100 more. The smugglers now have _____ parrots. These birds are crowded into very small cages. For many days they go without much food, water, or care. Out of every five birds one dies. Now there are _____ birds left. It is illegal to take parrots out of the country. In order to smuggle the parrots to the next country, the smugglers tape the beaks shut so they can't make noise. Their feet are tied together and each is wrapped in a newspaper. They are stuffed in a box. This careless handling kills 30 more birds. There are now _____ birds. A waiting dealer buys the box of birds even though it is against the law to do so. False information is written on the shipping records. The birds are shipped to a warehouse in your country. During the trip 20 more die. The remaining birds are purchased by pet stores where more careless handling kills 10 birds. Only _____ birds end up for sale in pet stores. A very nice family comes to buy a parrot. They admire its beauty and intelligence. They do not realize their purchase helps bring about the extinction of these parrots. Parrots do not have many offspring in any one year. So the flock of birds left in the jungle may never be able to build up their numbers. Even the parrot that goes home with the nice people may not live. It might be weak or ill and may die because of the change in climate.

Answers on last page

Captive breeding of animals and propagation of plants help to protect endangered species in the wild.

# Products-Beware!

Products made from endangered species are pictured below. **Match the product with one or more endangered species from which it is made.**

1. American Crocodile

2. African Elephant

3. Black Rhinoceros

4. Coral

5. Hawksbill Sea Turtle

6. Jaguar

7. Python Snake

8. Sperm Whale

A

B    Fertilizer

C    Yum Dog Food    Cream

D

E

F    Soup

G    medicine

Laws and international treaties make it a crime for travelers to bring these products into our country. Every one of these products can now be produced without using endangered species. Products are replaceable. Endangered species are not.

Answers on last page

# Wrong Place - Wrong Time

When people and animals use the same limited space, accidents happen. Cars, boats, and other vehicles can injure or kill wildlife. At least one Florida panther is killed each year by a car. Since probably fewer than 35 Florida panthers exist in the wild, traffic deaths are a major threat to this endangered animal. Propellers and keels on boats are a hazard for the Florida manatee. The manatee is a large, sea mammal that lives in shallow coastal waters also used by boaters.

## Florida Panther or Cougar

Length: up to 7 feet (2 meters) from nose to to tip of tail; females smaller

Weight: males up to 148 pounds (67 kg) females up to 100 pounds (45 kg)

Color: tawny brown back,; lower chest, belly, and inner legs lighter

Food: deer, wild hogs, raccoon, otter rabbits,cotton rats, armadillos, birds, insects,and even alligators

Habitat: once in many habitats of Florida and SE United States; now only in southern Florida

Reasons Endangered: killed by highway traffic, habitat loss, illegal hunting, overhunting, decrease of food

## West Indian (Florida) Manatee

Length: up to 13 feet (about 4 meters)

Weight: up to 1496 pounds (679 kg)

Color: dull gray to black

Food: sea grass and other water plants

Habitat: coastal waters and connecting rivers from the Carolinas, Georgia and Florida to northern Brazil

Reasons Endangered: collisions with motor boats and barges, habitat loss from silting of their feeding grounds, hunting in some countries

# Wheels of Misfortune

Certain materials are dangerous to plants and animals. When they are found in the wrong place, or in the wrong amounts, they can cause great harm to plants, animals, and people. These harmful materials are called **pollutants**.

**Look closely at the four wheels of misfortune. Which kind of pollution does each wheel show? Write the name of the pollutant on the line below the wheel.**

CHOICES:     1. Chemicals     2. Spills     3. Garbage     4. Acid Rain

A _____

B _____

C _____

D _____

Answers on last page

# Traveling Troubles

Migration is a regular seasonal journey from one area to another. Animals that migrate long distances always face more dangers than stay-at-homes. Storms, droughts, and predators are threats along the way. However, the biggest problem facing migratory animals today is due to the growing population of people and their actions. **Match the rhymes below with the migratory animals they describe.**

1. _____
Swimming from cold-water feeding grounds
To warm-water breeding grounds
This gentle giant faces many ills
From plastic garbage to oil spills.

2. _____
Flying South for the winter to stay alive
Avoiding many dangers to survive
Their wetland habitats drained and filled
Mistaken for game birds, they are often killed.

3. _____
Heading to sea from a nest on the beach
Dune buggies, collectors, buildings
make it hard to reach
Floating plastic bags look like a jelly fish meal
Getting caught in a shrimp net - What a rotten deal!

4. _____
On delicate wings they seek mountain forest trees
Where the temperature is just the right degrees
But farming and logging through last year's summer
Have changed their winter habitat - What a Bummer!

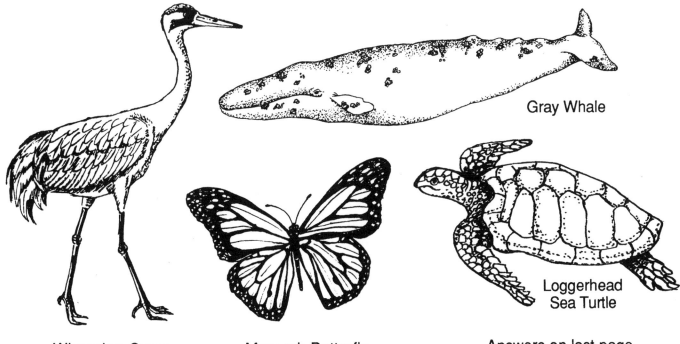

Gray Whale

Whooping Crane          Monarch Butterfly          Loggerhead
                                                    Sea Turtle

Answers on last page

29

# Risky Business

Some plants and animals are more likely to become endangered than others. Look at the paired pictures below. **Circle the one which is most at risk.**

The snail kite eats only apple snails

The raccoon eats a variety of food.

Salmon have lots of babies at one time.

Whales do not have many babies at once.

Black-capped chickadees stay in the same area all year.

Whooping cranes migrate to another area during winter.

Kirtland warblers live in jack-pine trees in Michigan.

Starlings live in a variety of habitats.

A dandelion is not wanted by collectors.

A green pitcher plant is wanted by collectors.

Mosquitoes get along fine even if change occurs.

The greenback cutthroat trout has trouble adjusting to change.

List the reasons you found which make an animal or plant more likely to become endangered.

Answers on last page

# Who Is More Important?

# Conservation Worldwide

Nations, states, private organizations, and individuals have set aside areas of land for wildlife and plants. These **protected areas** help maintain endangered species. They are also safe places for many other plants and animals that are not endangered. There are many kinds of protected areas. National parks, wildlife refuges, forests, ecological reserves, biosphere reserves and Nature Conservancy reserves are just a few.

 Help endangered and threatened species find their protected areas in the countries listed below. **Using a map of the world, write the name of the country and/or state on the correct line.** At each location you will find one protected species. Turn to the answer page and find the name of a specific preserve in each location.

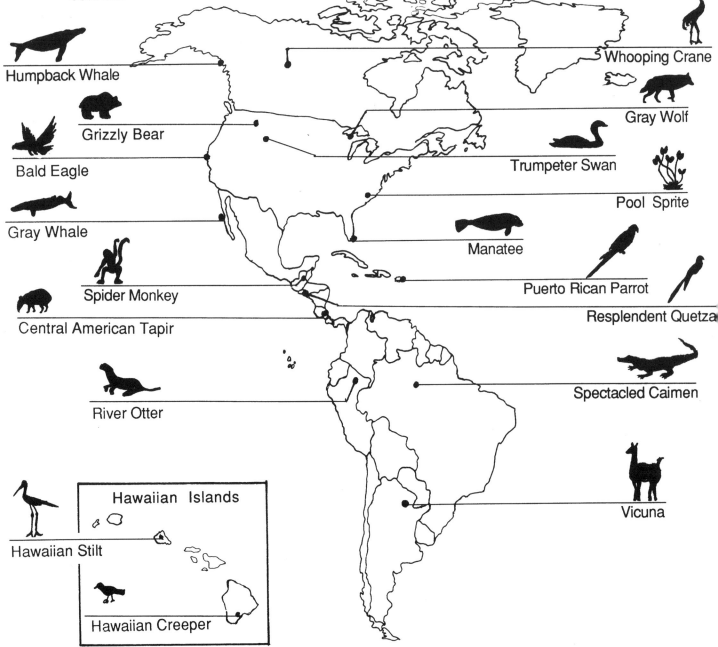

Humpback Whale

Grizzly Bear

Bald Eagle

Gray Whale

Spider Monkey

Central American Tapir

River Otter

Whooping Crane

Gray Wolf

Trumpeter Swan

Pool Sprite

Manatee

Puerto Rican Parrot

Resplendent Quetzal

Spectacled Caimen

Vicuna

Hawaiian Islands

Hawaiian Stilt

Hawaiian Creeper

Argentina
Australia
Botswana
Brazil
Burma
Canada
China
Costa Rica
El Salvador
England

France
Greece
Ghana
Guatemala
Kenya
Madagascar
Mexico
Nepal
New Guinea
Peru

Puerto Rico
Rwanda
South Africa
Tanzania
USA, Alaska
USA, California
USA, Florida
USA, Hawaii Island, Hawaii
USA, Oahu Island, Hawaii
USA, Michigan

USA, Montana
USA, South Carolina
USA, Wyoming
USSR
Vietnam
Zaire
Zimbabwe

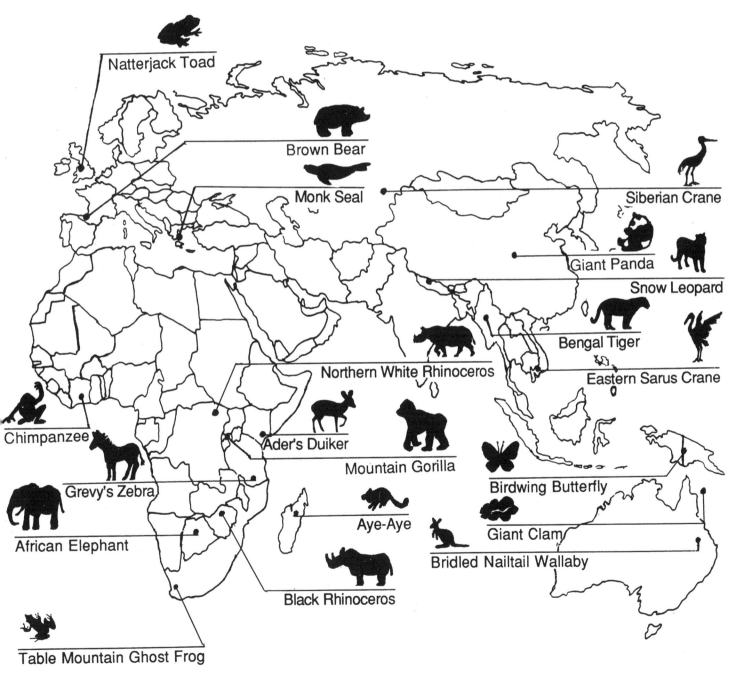

Natterjack Toad

Brown Bear

Monk Seal

Siberian Crane

Giant Panda

Snow Leopard

Bengal Tiger

Eastern Sarus Crane

Northern White Rhinoceros

Chimpanzee

Ader's Duiker

Mountain Gorilla

Birdwing Butterfly

Grevy's Zebra

Aye-Aye

Giant Clam

African Elephant

Bridled Nailtail Wallaby

Black Rhinoceros

Table Mountain Ghost Frog

# Making A Comeback

The problems facing endangered species are complicated. Solutions are not easy. Yet people want to help. Laws and international treaties protecting endangered animals and plants are helpful. Refuges and parks have been set up. **Reintroduction programs** put rare animals and plants back where they once lived. Because of these and other efforts, life is better now for some species. This doesn't mean they are completely out of danger. There are continuing threats to their survival in the future.

## American Alligator

Much of the alligator's habitat was destroyed by development. Many alligators were hunted for their skin to make shoes, purses, and belts. When they were declared endangered, it became illegal to hunt them. Land was set aside for their survival. Their numbers have now grown.

## Whooping Crane

At one time there were only 19 cranes left in the wild due to habitat loss and accidental hunting. Wood Buffalo National Park in Canada protects the nesting area. Aransas National Wildlife Refuge on the golf Coast of Texas in the U.S. protects the wintering site.

Scientists also have helped breed more cranes in captivity. A non-migratory flock was introduced in Florida. By1999 there were about 180 birds in the wild.

## Bald Eagle

Today it is illegal to hunt or kill the American national symbol. They were once killed as pests because they ate farm animals. Pesticides, pollution, and habitat destruction also reduced their numbers.

Laws to ban pesticides and clean up rivers have helped the eagle. So have reintroduction programs. Eagles are making a strong comeback. Once near extinction, the bald eagle is being removed from the endangered species list.

## Saved From Endangered Species List

As numbers increase, each animal or plant's situation changes. They may move from an endangered species to a threatened species. In some places, they will go off the endangered species list altogether.

Through careful conservation we are saving a precious handful. Other animals on the comeback trail include the cougar, koala, Florida key deer, trumpeter swam, elephant seal, peregrine falcon, golden lion tamarin, and wolf.

Keep track of animals and plants that are removed from the endangered species list.

| Species | Date | Place |
| --- | --- | --- |
| | | |
| | | |
| | | |
| | | |
| | | |
| | | |
| | | |
| | | |
| | | |
| | | |

# Floods and Arks

Do you know the legend of Noah's ark? One version tells how Noah carried seven pairs of each kind of animal on his ark to protect them from a big flood. Zoos, aquariums, and botanical gardens are like arks. They help to manage and protect endangered species from the flood of problems on our planet. They plan to do this until some future time when the world might be a healthier and safer place for the animals to live. This could take a few centuries or more.

**Can you fill this ark with some of your favorite endangered species?**

# What Can We Do?

My big sister is studying something called habitat restoration. She'll show us how to plant a yard for wildlife.

Maybe we can get a person from the nature center or science museum to come and talk to our class.

I am going to tell my parents to vote for laws to protect these animals, plants and habitats.

We can write elected representatives about saving endangered species and habitats.

Let's visit the parks, forests, and wildlife refuges in our country and learn about their problems.

Let's help the zoo plant trees. Plants are necessary for a healthy planet.

Let's join conservation organizations. There are many groups that help protect wildlife and wild places.

Good idea! Some of them have adoption programs. We could save our money and adopt a whale or other endangered animal.

Grevy's Zebra

# Protective Custody

Some species numbers are so low, a few or all the remaining members have been captured to help them survive. Several methods are used to help animals have offspring. Rare plants are propagated. They are grown from seeds or cuttings in greenhouses.

Captive breeding is the last hope for California condors. In 1987, the last bird was captured. At that time, there were only 27 California condors left in the world. In 1988, the first condor chick was hatched. Special habitat is being set aside for their reintroduction to the wild.

Pictured below are several endangered and threatened species we are trying to help. Each picture has a number. **Write the name of the animal or plant by its number in the puzzle. Rearrange the letters in the heavy squares.** You will find a mystery message from these species to you.

NAMES TO CHOOSE:
- California Condor
- Peregrine Falcon
- Red Wolf
- Black Footed Ferret
- Knowlton's Cactus
- American Bison

1. ___ ___ ___ ___ ___ ___ ___ ___ ___ ___ ___ ___ ___ ___ ___ ___

2. ___ ___ ___ ___ ___ ___ ___ ___ ___ ___ ___ ___ ___ ___

3. ___ ___ ___ ___ ___ ___ ___ ___ ___ ___ ___ ___ ___

4. ___ ___ ___ ___ ___ ___ ___ ___

5. ___ ___ ___ ___ ___ ___ ___ ___ ___ ___ ___ ___

6. ___ ___ ___ ___ ___ ___ ___ ___ ___ ___ ___ ___ ___

Mystery Message: ☐☐☐☐☐☐☐ ☐☐

38

# My Plan

This is my plan for helping with the endangered species problem:

_____

_____

_____

_____

_____

_____

_____

_____

_____

_____

_____

_____

_____

_____

_____

_____

_____

_____

_____

_____

_____

_____

Lange's Metalmark Butterfly    Oregon Silverspot Butterfly    Mission Blue Butterfly    Schaus Swallowtail Butterfly

# Brain Busters

1. Name some laws and treaties that help protect endangered species
2. What mammals are in trouble because they are caught in tuna fishing nets?
3. What foods come from tropical forests?
4. How many plants have edible parts? How many do people use for food?
5. How many species of ants have been found on one tropical forest tree?
6. How many animals also use the burrow made by a gopher tortoise? Would they be in trouble if the tortoise became extinct?
7. Why are California condors endangered?
8. What bats in the United States are endangered? Why?
9. What plant has been used to treat childhood leukemia and other cancers?

Answers are upside-down at the bottom of the page.

Spotted Dolphin

Gopher Tortoise

Eastern Indigo Snake

## Answers

p. 6 Earth's Gifts   A. Food  B. Products  C. Recreation  D. Medicine  E. Fuel  F. Clothes  G. Fertilize Flowers  H. Beauty
   I. Make Oxygen                         p. 7 Bricks of the Earth :   Between bricks 10 to 14 the house would fall down.

p. 8 What Do Living things Need? OWL: Food 5 and 6, Water 9 or 4, Nest Site 1 or 2, SALAMANDER: Food 7 and 8, Water
   3 ,Shelter 3,  SQUIRREL:  Food 12, Water 4 or 9, Nest Site  2, HEMLOCK SEEDLING: Place to Grow 3, Place to get
   Nutrients 3,  Water 3,  FALSE LADY'S SLIPPER: Place to Grow 10, Place to get  Nutrients 10, Water 10.

p. 10 What Goes Wrong?  A.  Original habitat  B.  Lumber cut for buildings, firewood and furniture  C.  Agriculture, clearing land for
   farms  D.  Draining and filling wetlands  E.  Construction of dams  F.  Growth of cities.

p. 14 Rain Forests

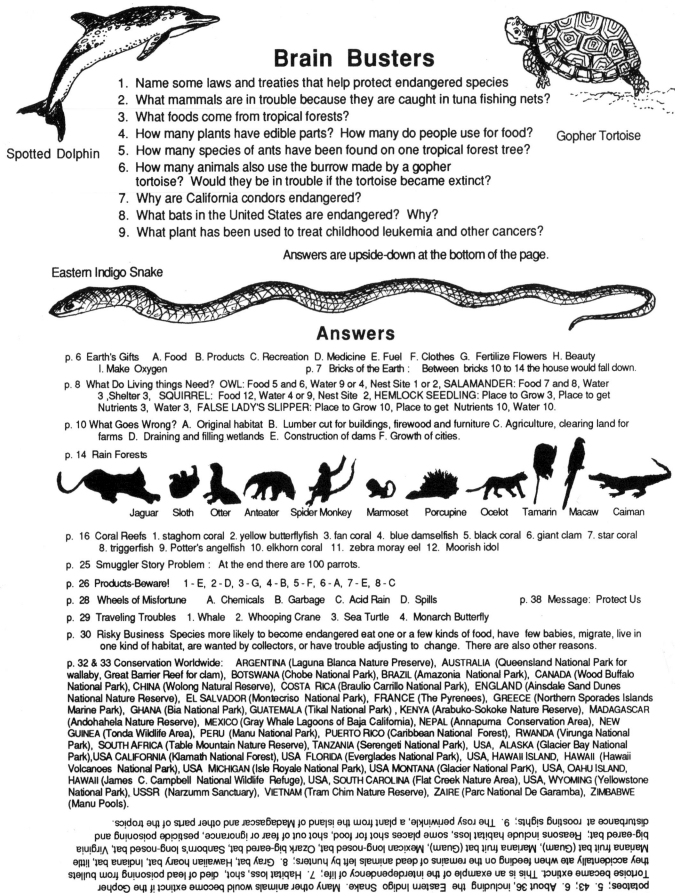

Jaguar   Sloth   Otter   Anteater   Spider Monkey   Marmoset   Porcupine   Ocelot   Tamarin   Macaw   Caiman

p. 16 Coral Reefs 1. staghorn coral  2. yellow butterflyfish  3. fan coral  4. blue damselfish  5. black coral  6. giant clam  7. star coral
   8. triggerfish  9. Potter's angelfish  10. elkhorn coral  11. zebra moray eel  12. Moorish idol

p. 25 Smuggler Story Problem :  At the end there are 100 parrots.

p. 26 Products-Beware!    1 - E,  2 - D,  3 - G,  4 - B,  5 - F,  6 - A,  7 - E,  8 - C

p. 28  Wheels of Misfortune     A. Chemicals  B. Garbage  C. Acid Rain  D. Spills          p. 38  Message:  Protect Us

p. 29  Traveling Troubles  1. Whale  2. Whooping Crane  3. Sea Turtle  4. Monarch Butterfly

p. 30  Risky Business  Species more likely to become endangered eat one or a few kinds of food, have few babies, migrate, live in
   one kind of habitat, are wanted by collectors, or have trouble adjusting to change.  There are also other reasons.

p. 32 & 33 Conservation Worldwide:   ARGENTINA (Laguna Blanca Nature Preserve), AUSTRALIA (Queensland National Park for
wallaby, Great Barrier Reef for clam), BOTSWANA (Chobe National Park), BRAZIL (Amazonia  National Park), CANADA (Wood Buffalo
National Park), CHINA (Wolong Natural Reserve), COSTA RICA (Braulio Carrillo National Park), ENGLAND (Ainsdale Sand Dunes
National Nature Reserve), EL SALVADOR (Montecriso  National Park), FRANCE (The Pyrenees), GREECE (Northern Sporades Islands
Marine Park), GHANA (Bia National Park), GUATEMALA (Tikal National Park) , KENYA (Arabuko-Sokoke Nature Reserve), MADAGASCAR
(Andohahela Nature Reserve), MEXICO (Gray Whale Lagoons of Baja California), NEPAL (Annapurna  Conservation Area),  NEW
GUINEA (Tonda Wildlife Area),  PERU (Manu National Park),  PUERTO RICO (Caribbean National  Forest),  RWANDA (Virunga National
Park),  SOUTH AFRICA (Table Mountain Nature Reserve), TANZANIA (Serengeti National Park), USA,  ALASKA (Glacier Bay National
Park),USA CALIFORNIA (Klamath National Forest), USA  FLORIDA (Everglades National Park), USA, HAWAII ISLAND, HAWAII  (Hawaii
Volcanoes  National Park), USA MICHIGAN (Isle Royale National Park), USA MONTANA (Glacier National Park),  USA, OAHU ISLAND,
HAWAII (James  C. Campbell  National Wildlife  Refuge), USA, SOUTH CAROLINA (Flat Creek Nature Area), USA, WYOMING (Yellowstone
National Park), USSR  (Narzumm Sanctuary),  VIETNAM (Tram Chim Nature Reserve),  ZAIRE (Parc National De Garamba), ZIMBABWE
(Manu Pools).

BRAIN BUSTERS: 1. Endangered Species Act, an international treaty called CITIES (Convention on International Trade in Endangered Species of Wild Fauna and Flora), Lacy Act, Marine Mammal Protection Act, Migratory Bird Treaty Act; 2. Dolphins; 3. Foods include chocolate, cola, banana, coffee, cashew nuts, Brazil nuts, macadamia nuts coconut, avocado, orange, papaya fruit, pineapple, plantain, grapefruit, guava fruit, passion fruit,and many spices like black pepper, chili pepper, cinnamon, cloves, ginger, mace, nutmeg and paprika; 4. At least 75,000; People use 7000, with heavy reliance on 20 such as wheat, corn, rice and potatoes; 5. 43; 6. About 36. Many other animals would become extinct if the Gopher Tortoise became extinct. This is an example of the interdependency of life; 7. Habitat loss, shot, died of lead poisoning from bullets they accidentally ate when feeding on the remains of dead animals left by hunters; 8. Gray bat, Hawaiian hoary bat, Indiana bat, little Mariana fruit bat (Guam), Mexican long-nosed bat, Ozark big-eared bat, Sanborn's long-nosed bat, Virginia big-eared bat; Reasons include habitat loss, some places shot for food, shot out of fear or ignorance, pesticide poisoning and disturbance at roosting sights; 9. The rosy periwinkle, a plant from the island of Madagascar and other parts of the tropics.

40